The Art Of Dialogue Writing

For Middle School & High School

Written by:
Stacey Cotrufo

©2011 Stacey Cotrufo

Table of Contents

- Introduction

- Lesson One: Basic Dialogue Structure and Punctuation

- Lesson Two: Knowing the People Behind the Dialogue

- Lesson Three: How Demographics Shape the Way We Speak

- Lesson Four: Setting the Scene

- Lesson Five: More than he said/she said

- Lesson Six: Voice/Action/Reaction within Dialogue

- Lesson Seven: Emotional Dialogue

- Lesson Eight: Interview With a Friend

- Lesson Nine: When to Use Dialogue

- Lesson Ten: The Voices in Your Head: Inner Dialogue

- Lesson Eleven: A Complete Scene

©2011 Stacey Cotrufo

INTRODUCTION – THE ART OF DIALOGUE WRITING

Welcome to "The Art of Dialogue Writing"!

This workbook is designed to help you, young writers, learn the process of writing clear and interesting dialogue within your fictional stories.

Writing dialogue is a rather complex part of the story telling process because it is not only about what is being said but *how* things are being said. Dialogue reveals someone's character and the relationship between characters. No two people speak alike and you should try to give your characters a verbal as well as a physical distinctiveness. Do they use a certain turn of phrase? A slang word? A swear word? Do they stutter or say 'um' and 'ah' a lot? These are some of the things that would come across in your dialogue writing and things that you would have to remember about each character that you are writing about so that you stay true to the people you created throughout your story.

The workbook will cover these topic lessons:

- Basic dialogue writing/construction
- Knowing who is speaking
- Emotional dialogue
- Setting the scene
- Character background
- Giving your character a voice
- And so much more!

By the end of the book, you will be able to express some clearly written dialogue within any story that you write. In any fictional story, dialogue is included and this dialogue – whether it is witty, emotional, angry or just there as page filler – needs to be written in a way that the reader can understand exactly who is speaking and what kind of emotion you are trying to portray in your scene. It may sound easy but how your paragraphs are structured and how your dialogue is laid out on the page can either enhance your story or confuse your reader to the point that they no longer want to read what you've written.

©Stacey Cotrufo

The Art of Dialogue Writing   Introduction – pg. 2

So here's me:

Stacey Cotrufo is a married, mother of two freelance writer from Wake Forest, North Carolina who self-published her first novel in 2011 and since that time has gone on to release twenty-two books! During that time she was also signed by a major publisher for a twelve-book deal. Her freelance work can be seen on Examiner.com, eHow, Bukisa.com, The Mouse for Less Guest Blog as well as in the Wake Weekly newspaper. She has taught various writing classes to the homeschool community for more than ten years and her classes have included: Creative writing, literary essay writing, research paper writing and more personalized workshops such as dialogue writing and character developing. Stacey is currently writing contemporary romance and has been an active participant in National Novel Writing Month (NaNoWriMo) and Amazon's Breakthrough Novel Award contests and was a top five finalist in the International contest of Harlequin's Editor's Pitch Challenge.

Take a moment and describe yourself. How would you introduce yourself if you were being interviewed?

_____

_____

_____

_____

_____

_____

©Stacey Cotrufo

The Art of Dialogue Writing

How to Use this Book

This curriculum was originally designed as a four-week workshop with the lessons posted on Mondays, Wednesdays and Fridays. With the workbook format, you are free to use this as you see fit and spread out the lessons however you want. Each lesson will require some sort of action by you, the student, but most of the assignments will be brief and easy for you to work on. This was how it was done as an on-line format:

Week #1:
Monday – Introduction
Wednesday – Basic Dialogue Structure and Punctuation
Friday – Knowing the People Behind the Dialogue

Week #2:
Monday – How Demographics Shape the Way We Speak
Wednesday – Setting the Scene
Friday – More than he said/she said

Week #3:
Monday – Voice/Action/Reaction within Dialogue
Wednesday – Emotional Dialogue
Friday – Interview with a Friend

Week #4:
Monday – When to Use Dialogue
Wednesday – The Voices in Your Head: Inner Dialogue
Friday - A Complete Scene

This is just an example of how to divide up the topics. If you want to use the book five days a week, that will work. If you would only like to use the book once a week, that will work too! Being that creative writing is not usually something done as a primary subject, you fit it in to your schedule wherever you see fit.

©2011 Stacey Cotrufo

HOMEWORK:

As I stated earlier, I believe that you will get the most out of this workbook if you actively participate in the assignments. With each lesson there will be a homework assignment for you to complete. The purpose of this is for you to put in to practice what we are discussing. If you do all of the exercises and assignments, by the end of the book you will have a solid foundation be able to sit down and creatively write almost anything.

The thing to remember is that when you are writing creatively, there are no right or wrong answers; it is all what you have created in your mind. Share your work with a parent, your family or friends and get their feedback! Don't be ashamed of what you've done, sometimes getting feedback from others enhances the creative process!

Most importantly, just keep writing. Do all of the assignments and whether you do them here in the book or on computer or wherever it is that you feel comfortable, just be sure to get your ideas down on paper. If you need to step away from your work for a day or two, that's okay. Never get discouraged because you can do anything that you put your mind to!

Getting Started!

What type of stories do you like to read? What type of stories do you think you'd like to write? Take a moment and write that out below. Remember to use full sentences and tell why you enjoy this type of genre.

_____
_____
_____
_____
_____

©2011 Stacey Cotrufo

The Art of Dialogue Writing

Basic Dialogue Structure and Punctuation

Dialogue is an important part of any fiction story. In most cases you have more than one character in your story and at some point, they are going to have to communicate. Throughout most of this workshop we are going to go from the position of having one-on-one conversation/dialogue. There will be times, however, where we will introduce a third or fourth character in to the mix but for the most part, our dialogue will be between two people.

Having said that, you can have a GREAT conversation in your head that you want to use in your story. You may have thought out who is saying what, and how they are going to say it; you can have the whole thing pictured in your mind but if it is not properly written on the page, your reader is going to be thoroughly confused.

Now, I am a creative writer and what I have found is that creative writing is a little less formal than other forms of writing. In creative fiction writing, some of the grammar and punctuation rules that you grew up learning do not apply. This is not to say that you can forget them all and just put anything down on the page; far from it. BUT you will find that it is okay to use a fragment sentence or if there is verb confusion or some such thing that Microsoft Word may pop up a warning about, it's okay. Do not freak out when one of those warnings pop up because you can choose to ignore it.

If you listen to conversations around you or really think about a conversation that you are having with someone, you will see that we all do not use proper English all of the time so why would your characters? We are not perfect and so chances are that our characters aren't going to be, either.

So keeping that in mind, this lesson will be the most structured of them all because in this one we are going to go over the "rules" of writing and punctuating dialogue. I will bold-print the rule and then give you an example of what I mean by that rule – the bold print will help you use it for quick reference in the future.

Are we ready to dig in??

©Stacey Cotrufo

The Art of Dialogue Writing

Always use quotation marks to begin and end a direct quotation. Use a comma to separate who is speaking from what is being said.

James said, "I won't be able to make it to the movies tonight." OR
"I won't be able to make it to the movies tonight," James said.

If a question mark or exclamation point occurs where one of the separating commas should be, delete the comma and use the question mark or exclamation point to separate the material.

"I won't be able to make it to the movies tonight!" James yelled.

Always capitalize the first word in the quotation.

*He said, "**W**e'll find another time to go and hang out."*

If you divide your quotation in half by interjecting who is speaking, use a capital letter to start the sentence but you do not capitalize again until a new sentence starts.

"I won't be able to make it to the movies tonight," James said, "because I have to go to work."

"I won't be able to make it to the movies tonight," James sighed. "My boss called me in to work."

*See the difference between those two examples? In the first one, I put who was speaking in the middle of the quote whereas in the second one, I put who was speaking between two separate sentences.

Periods and commas ALWAYS go INSIDE the quotation marks.

"I wish I was on vacation right now," Nick said.

Nick said, "I wish I was on vacation right now."

©Stacey Cotrufo

When you write dialogue, always begin a new paragraph whenever the speaker changes.

"I'd say we are more than done, Mr. Lawrence." She was proud of the fact that her voice sounded steady and that she had her temper under control. "CJ's has enjoyed providing our service for all of your events for the last two years but this is one time that I simply cannot meet your request. It's unreasonable of you to ask that we change the entire menu on such short notice. If you'd like to find another event planner and caterer that is your prerogative."

"I don't want another event planner, Cassandra," Adam replied irritably. "We have a contract; one that states that changes can be made…"

"Up to two weeks before," she cut in with frustration.

"The L.S.S. Fall Retreat is two weeks away," he replied mildly, clearly believing to have the upper hand. His confidence tipped a bit when he noticed Cassie had her own triumphant smile as she reached in to her leather brief case.

Pulling out her day planner, Cassie opened to September's calendar and turned it to face Adam. "Today is the twelfth; your retreat is on the twenty-third. That is eleven days, not two weeks."

Use a series of three dots (Ellipsis Points) to indicate an abrupt break in thought or speech or an unfinished statement or question.

"First of all," he said, "we have a contract, Cassandra, and it clearly states that I have the option of changing the menu. If you'll recall…"

"Changes can be made up to two weeks before," she cut in with frustration.

"…and the L.S.S. Fall Retreat is only two weeks away!" Adam finished, equally frustrated.

*In some grammar books, you will be told to use an em dash (which is a series of two dashes) but I prefer the three dots method.

©Stacey Cotrufo

The Art of Dialogue Writing   Lesson One – pg. 8

If you have the same person (character) saying lengthy dialogue, you may choose to keep everything in one paragraph or separate parts in to their own paragraphs. Make this decision using the same criteria you would use in deciding to start a new paragraph without dialogue in it. Meaning, if your character is talking about several different topics, give each one their own paragraph. Always make sure, however, that you make it clear who is speaking at all times.

AND

When a speaker's words run for more than one paragraph, use quotation marks at the beginning of the quotation, at the beginning of each paragraph, and at the end of the whole quotation.

"I don't see how you can expect me to make these changes on such short notice, Mr. Lawrence," Cassie said. "We had an agreement. I have organized this event based on that agreement and asking me to change that at this point would create a lot of extra work for me!"

"Besides that, we have a legally binding contract. You are asking me to break the contract when in fact it is you, sir, who is breaking it."

"I hardly see where that is the case," he said.

"Trust me, I've been dealing with this sort of thing for years and what you are doing is breaking the contract by asking me to make these changes. If you'd like to ask your lawyer…?"

"That won't be necessary, Cassandra," Adam said quietly, "we'll continue with things as they are."

Okay, I know that there was a lot of information there but for the most part, this is all stuff that you probably have learned in your English and Language Art lessons over the years. Don't let dialogue writing scare you; just remember how to separate it within your story and to keep it clear as to who is speaking at all times.

©Stacey Cotrufo

The Art of Dialogue Writing   Lesson One – pg. 9

Exercise One:

Using each of the eight rules listed above, write out dialogue of your own. You can do it as one big dialogue or do it as one example for each, the choice is yours. PLEASE remember to keep the dialogue between only TWO people.

_____

_____

_____

_____

_____

_____

_____

The Art of Dialogue Writing

The Art of Dialogue Writing   Lesson Two – pg. 11

Knowing the People Behind the Dialogue

For those of you who have taken my workshop on Character Development, this lesson will be a breeze! It won't be hard for the rest of you either, so please don't worry!

Okay, in order to have really great dialogue, it helps if you really know the people who are doing the talking. What we did yesterday in lesson one was fine – you were just using generic people to demonstrate that you knew how to apply the rules of writing dialogue. From now on, however, I want you to have two very specific characters that you are going to use for all of our dialogue writing.

So basically, we are going to take a one-month workshop that I did and over-simplify it in to one day.

No problem, right?

Where do we begin? For starters, you need to create two characters. If you already have a story that you are working on, then choose characters from there. If you do not have a work in progress, you are going to start from scratch and create two characters.

We need to have some basic information on these characters to work from. All of this information may not ever come up in any dialogue that you write for them, but we all have a background and personality that makes us who we are and makes us speak and react the way that we do. By giving your character a little history and background, it will help you as the writer understand how they would speak and react during any kind of conversation.

For example: If I grew up poor, there is no way that I could have any real kind of conversation about "summering in Europe" or be able to share my thoughts on going to a private school. Sure, these are topics that can come up and my responses would probably consist of "I have no idea" and that doesn't make for interesting dialogue at all!

©Stacey Cotrufo

The Art of Dialogue Writing   Lesson Two – pg. 12

We are going to take this process of fleshing out your characters step-by-step. The first step is to give them a detailed history. You are going to take both characters and give a detailed history of their life. Some of things you can include are:
- How old are they?
- Where are they from?
- Do they have siblings?
- How big is their family?
- What are some of their likes and dislikes and why?
- A brief physical description
- Give them at least ONE traumatic incident from their childhood
- Who influences them and why?
- What is their job/career? (if they are an adult)
- What are their hobbies? Talents?
- Give them at least one embarrassing moment
- What is their highest education and what did they study?
- What is their relationship like with their best friend?
- What are they afraid of?
- What makes them happy?

I want to take a moment and briefly discuss physical descriptions. Sometimes your dialogue will consist of inner dialogue – what someone is thinking in their head – and sometimes that will deal with the physical description of the person they are talking to. This is the reason why we will need more than a general description.

Most of us don't have something that obvious or remarkable about ourselves or something about our physical attributes that would make us stand out that much in a crowd. Don't think that you have to go over the top with how your characters look. Most of us are pretty ordinary looking but it is what is on the inside that counts. Ordinary is fine. Ordinary is great. BUT (and I emphasize this) you will need to think beyond the "brown hair, brown eyes, tan and thin. Five feet two inches tall, medium build description.

This would be a GREAT description if they were wanted by the police and they just wanted the basics to put out their APB. But you are writing a great story about an interesting character. How can you improve on that description so that this person jumps off the page?

©Stacey Cotrufo

The Art of Dialogue Writing   Lesson Two –pg. 13

There is a way to state things that can make it sound more interesting, as well. For example, not everyone with brown hair has plain brown hair. You can use phrases like "rich brown", "mahogany", "chestnut", "light brown", "dark brown", etc. The same can be said with eye color – it's not always cut and dried on what shade of color someone's eyes are. Blue eyes come in many different shades and the more specific you write, the more your reader will be able to clearly picture your character in their minds as they read your stories.

I know it seems odd to focus on that when we're talking about *TALKING* but really, writing dialogue will become much easier when you are completely familiar with the people that you are writing about.

Exercise Two:

First I want you to look in the mirror and write up a thorough physical description of yourself. BE DESCRIPTIVE!

_____

_____

_____

_____

_____

The Art of Dialogue Writing   Lesson Two –pg. 14

Next I want you to write and equally descriptive piece on both of your characters.

_____

_____

_____

_____

_____

_____

_____

And finally, I want you to write up your character's history's using the 15 questions above as a guideline. You can use other bits of information not listed but I want you to give as much information as possible.

_____

_____

_____

_____

_____

_____

_____

©2011 Stacey Cotrufo

How Demographics Shape the Way We Speak

East coast, west coast. North, South, Yankee or Southerner. Right side of the tracks, wrong side of the tracks. City or suburbs. Public school, private school, home school? Believe it or not, all of these things factor in to the type of people we are and how we speak.

If you were born and raised in the same home, the same town and never experienced life anywhere else then some of this may be a revelation for you. Where you live, where you grew up and where you went to school plays a big part in the person you are.

For example: I grew up on Long Island. The island itself is not very large. I mean, it is *long* (about 120 miles) but not very wide (about 20 miles). But we were part of New York and if you've ever been there or ever met anyone from there, you know that New Yorkers have a very distinct accent. I speak fast, I speak loud and there is most definitely the accent. People only have to hear me say a few words before they ask "Are you from New York?'

When we moved from Long Island to North Carolina, I was shocked by the differences. Not only did we *sound* different but the foods were different, the fashions were slightly different, the schooling was different, the climate was different...it was amazing. And it wasn't only the way we sounded that was different it was phrases and words that were different. Up North, you would never address someone as "Miss Stacey"; up there I was either Mrs. Cotrufo or just plain Stacey. That took a little getting used to.

No matter where you go, not only in this country but all over the world, people will sound different. Even within the same state, like here in North Carolina, different regions have different accents. It may seem strange but there it is. New York and Massachusetts are not far apart but you can definitely tell the difference between a New York accent and a Boston accent. Someone who is from Texas sounds completely different from someone from Florida even though they are both at the most Southern point of the United States.

©2011 Stacey Cotrufo

The Art of Dialogue Writing   Lesson Three – pg. 17

When you are creating your character and deciding where they live and where they grew up, you are going to need to research that area so that your character stays true to form. Someone who grew up in the South is going to have a Southern accent and going to say things like "Y'all" whereas a New Yorker would *never* say such a thing. Someone from Brooklyn, New York would have a very specific type of accent and mannerism that you aren't going to find in Nashville, Tennessee.

Someone who grew up with great wealth would carry themselves a bit differently in manners, etiquette and education and be more polished in the way that they speak than say someone who grew up very poor. These are things to look at and consider when you are trying to figure out how to write how someone speaks.

Researching a specific country, state, city, town, etc. can really make your character come alive. Knowing the dialect is something that will truly help you develop a well-rounded character.

Think about your own family. Where did your parents grow up? How about your grandparents? It is only a small percentage of the population where multiple generations have stayed in one spot. We tend to move around a lot. I was born and raised on Long Island but had moved a total of 12 times in 25 years! For the most part I stayed in a 20 square mile radius but before me, my parents lived more westward on the island. Now I'm in North Carolina, my dad is in Florida while my mom and sister stayed on the island.

My grandparents on my father's side were from Italy and still spoke Italian from time to time. It wasn't unusual growing up for us to speak a phrase or two in Italian and to this day there are certain words that we still say (mostly cooking phrases) that most people around us here in the South don't understand!

I am an Italian-American but I don't know enough Italian that I would use it in dialogue based on myself. I've read some books where the main character has some sort of foreign accent and to make it seem authentic, they'll throw in a phrase or two (usually an endearment) to remind the reader of the character's heritage. Sure, it works but at times it doesn't seem natural. Make sure if you try to do that, that the phrase fits the scene.

©2011 Stacey Cotrufo

The Art of Dialogue Writing   Lesson Three – pg. 18

Learning about other cultures is a good thing and while writing about what you know and are comfortable with is easy, doing a little research to help you create an amazing character can be a great experience and can help create some interesting dialogue.

Some other things to keep in mind, just as you wouldn't make two characters look the same (unless they're twins) you don't want to make any two characters sound exactly the same either. Even though people from the same part of the country or members of the same family may sound a lot alike (sharing speech patterns, vocabulary, and even expressions) they don't sound identical to each other and neither should your characters.

Don't let your own voice come through too much for every character that your write about. Your heroine, especially in your first book or story, may sound a lot like you but just make sure that every heroine in every book or story that you write also doesn't sound like you. Otherwise your readers might think that you can't actually CREATE a character!

Exercise 3:

Think about your characters. Where are they from and where are they living (where are they at) now as you are writing about them. Is there something about their dialect that is going to make them stand out? Do they have a certain phrase that is associated with where they live?

Next, I want you to write a normal, average conversation between your two characters so that we can see (read) how their background and nationality shines through in their conversation.

_____

_____

_____

_____

_____

©2011 Stacey Cotrufo

The Art of Dialogue Writing — Lesson Four – pg. 20

Setting the Scene for Your Dialogue

Imagine that you are walking though an art museum. You stroll through the rooms looking at classic works of art. There is classical music playing softly in the background. Would this be a place where you would be yelling out obnoxious jokes?

Hopefully not.

Or how about finding yourself at a formal dinner party. You're seated at a table for twenty and everyone is dressed in gowns and tuxedos; the tables are covered in snowy white linens. There are candles lit along the center of the table and the lighting in the room is dim. Would you shout to the person at the other end of the table to pass the salt because the food has no taste?

Let's hope not here, too.

There are places that we go where certain behavior, certain attire and a certain tone of voice are very important. If you've ever walked the halls of a hospital you'll notice people talking in hushed tones. In a movie theater, people whisper while other people tell them to be quiet. How much quieter can a whisper be?

It is completely acceptable to laugh loudly and often at an outdoor barbeque or at a festive party but it would be frowned upon at the above formal dinner. Telling raunchy stories in a bar is acceptable; telling them while sitting in a funeral parlor is not.

When you are writing a scene where two or more people are talking you have to take in to consideration WHERE they are before going and digging in to the dialogue and conversation. You can have them say what you want them to say no matter where they are, but you would have to be very specific in HOW they are saying it.

©Stacey Cotrufo

The Art of Dialogue Writing   Lesson Four – pg. 21

For example:

"I cannot believe that you chose to wear that dress here!" Tina shouted.

Clearly, she is yelling and a little bit angry. This would be an acceptable way of writing this sentence in a casual setting – like a restaurant, a party, a house.

"I cannot believe that you chose to wear that dress here!" Tina hissed in Sarah's ear.

The hissing in someone's ear would show that Tina did not want her statement overheard by anyone other than Sarah and while yes, that can still hold true in a casual setting, this would also work if they were someplace where yelling something like that out for the entire world to hear would not be acceptable.

"I cannot believe she chose to wear that dress here," Tina mumbled under her breath as Sarah walked across the room.

Again, not wanting to be heard by anyone (not even Sarah) and it shows her emotion, her dislike, maybe even her sarcasm and you could build a scene around that and future dialogue. Maybe someone heard what she mumbled and they would have a heated but quiet exchange of words off in the corner of a room or they'd take their discussion outside where they can be loud and yell if need be. It's your conversation and you can make it go anywhere that you want it to!

How we speak is effected by where we are at that moment. As I mentioned in yesterday's lesson, I speak loudly. It's just who I am. At work, however, I speak in a more subdued tone of voice. I often laugh on Sunday mornings because there are some people that specifically have a Sunday morning "church" voice. You know what I am talking about. Something about being in church makes people speak a little nice, a little more polite and with a little more graciousness than they do Monday through Saturday.

©Stacey Cotrufo

The Art of Dialogue Writing   Lesson Four – pg. 22

There was a comedian that I once saw who did this whole skit on how his mom talked. She would ask a question that was completely normal and spoken in a normal tone of voice but when she gave the answer, she whispered it. She would say something like, "Oh, did you hear about Mrs. Anderson?" in a completely normal tone of voice but then say "She has cancer" in a whisper. As if saying the negative bit of information in a whisper was going to help! I notice people doing that and it always makes me giggle a little.

Think about yourself. I know you're still young and you tend to be who you are wherever you are but try to put yourself in different scenarios. Do you speak the same way at home as you do at church? Do you speak to your parents the same way you speak to say a teacher or a friend's parents? Do you speak to a stranger the way you speak to your siblings?

Think about the volume level of your voice. Clearly when you are at the mall you have to speak louder than you would in the quiet of your living room. If you were in the middle of taking a dance class and you were doing ballet would you speak to the girl next to you in the same tone of voice that you would if you were practicing on the softball team and speaking to the girl over at second base? Probably not.

Be aware of your characters surroundings and have them act and speak accordingly.

Exercise 4:

You are going to write out dialogue for two different scenes. In the first one your characters are at home, hanging out and talking. The topic can be on anything that you want it to be but I want you to change speakers frequently and have them carry on a significant conversation. Do not give the type of dialogue where one of your characters only gives one word answers (unless they are mad at the other character and trying to annoy them!). Be creative and think about a conversation that you've had while just hanging out at home.

©Stacey Cotrufo

The Art of Dialogue Writing

In the second dialogue your characters are in a more formal environment – a museum, a church event, a funeral – someplace where they'd have to have a little bit more control over their tone of voice. Again, the conversation is completely up to you as the writer just make sure that it is a significant conversation where there is truly an exchange of words.

The Art of Dialogue Writing   Lesson Five – pg. 25

More Than He Said/She Said

"I'm hungry," Tom said.
"Me, too," John said.
"What do you think we should have?" Tom said.
"I think I want pizza," John said.
"I could go for that," Tom said.
"I'll call the order in," John said.

OH…MY…GOSH!!! Is that a boring conversation or what??? I mean, nobody talks like that, right? I hope not. By that little bit of conversation, all I can imagine are two guys sitting on a couch, staring at the walls and speaking in very monotone voices.

Boring!

When we speak, we are animated! We have facial expressions and inflections in our voice. We move around, we use our hands to gesture to things around us…we do NOT just sit still with our hands at our sides and stare straight ahead. We blink, we glare, we squint; our eyebrows raise, we smile, we smirk, we laugh. There are even times where we carry on conversations while doing something else!

These two guys in the conversation above? We can have them doing just about anything while this conversation is going on. And what's more, we can show HOW they say things instead of just saying "he said".

He said, she said, he yelled, she exclaimed, she cried, she signed, he said with a smile…these are just a few examples of how people say things. It really is rare that we just "say" – there is usually a tone, an inflection or an emotion that will tell anyone who is listening to us how we feel.

When you are on the phone with someone, you cannot see what they are doing. You have no idea what is going on in their head or read the emotion on their face because you cannot see them. Well, your reader cannot SEE how your character feels or what they think unless you convey it clearly in your writing.

©Stacey Cotrufo

If an entire book was written as plainly as that above dialogue, no one would even get past the first three pages and they certainly wouldn't suggest that book to a friend. The goal in writing a book is to get it published and read by the masses. In order for that to happen, you have to be able to write the kind of book that holds the readers attention and has your characters and their world coming alive off of the page.

By showing how something is being said and being able to convey the action and emotion behind it will truly make your scene come alive. With our above dialogue, here is another way that we could write that where it is a little more interesting.

> *With guns blazing and a mission to be won, Tom tapped furiously on his game controller in hopes of winning. "I'm hungry," he said, leaning forward in his seat.*
> *John waited until the enemy was blown apart before answering. "Yeah," he mumbled, his voice tight as a second enemy came out of nowhere on the screen, "me, too."*
> *With a growl of frustration, Tom continued his endless shooting. "What do you think we should have?"*
> *"I think I want pizza."*
> *Taking his thumbs off of the controller for a second to give them a break from the ruthless treatment he'd been giving them, Tom thought about the suggestion. "I could go for that."*
> *Throwing his controller down in disgust as his man went down, John stood. "I'll call the order in."*

See the difference? Their conversation was completely the same. Other than adding that "Yeah", I kept their words exactly the same. I added action and tone and I set the scene a little. If you've ever been in the room with a boy playing "Halo" or "Mortal Combat" you'll know that this is a rather familiar scene. Don't get me wrong, the conversation itself is boring, but with the right descriptions around it and with action, it makes it more visual in your mind.

©2011 Stacey Cotrufo

When you are writing a scene and you are ready to start writing your dialogue always remember that dialogue is not always just about WHAT is being said, it is also about HOW something is said and what is going on while it is being said.

So step away from the boring he said/she said and explore other ways of sharing your conversation.

Exercise 5:

This one has two parts. First, I want you to go and have a significant conversation with a member of your family. It doesn't matter who, just as long as there are some sentences exchanged. Observe how they speak – what do they do with their hands, their facial expressions as they speak, their tone of voice. What is going on around you while you are speaking. Take that experience and write it out for us using the rules of dialogue writing.

_____

_____

_____

_____

_____

_____

_____

_____

_____

Introduction to Creative Writing   Lesson 5 – pg. 28

_____

_____

_____

_____

_____

_____

_____

_____

Secondly, create a scene with your characters where action and setting play as important of a roll as the words. Have them doing something while having their conversation.

_____

_____

_____

_____

_____

_____

_____

_____

Introduction to Creative Writing — Lesson 5 – pg. 29

The Art of Dialogue Writing   Lesson Six – pg. 30

Voice/Actions/Reactions Within Dialogue
Less is more!

We're going to continue to build on what we talked about in lesson five because it is such an important concept and not including enough actions and reactions can be just as detrimental to a story as putting in too much information.

Too much information? Is that even possible?

YES!

Okay, if you are writing a scene in your book where there is dialogue, if you have been telling/writing your story thoroughly, it is not necessary to include who is speaking and how they are speaking/feeling at the end of every quote. Remember yesterday when I wrote that first really boring dialogue with Tom said, John said after each quote? Well, if that had gone on for a few more sentences wouldn't you – the reader – have caught on within the first few lines that this conversation was pretty much like a ping-pong ball going back and forth? Would I have really needed to keep adding Tom said, John said after each and every sentence?

I would hope not.

When you are new to dialogue writing, you tend to want to include EVERY emotion, thought, feeling, person speaking that you possibly can because you want to be thorough.

DON'T DO THAT.

It may sound fine while you are writing it but if you put that paper down for a little while and go back to it, you will find that it is overkill and sometimes verges on the ridiculous. Remember, if you have been breathing life in to these characters and writing an interesting and descriptive story, your reader should not have to be spoon fed every minute aspect like who is speaking and how they are saying it. They should KNOW because you have written it so well!

©Stacey Cotrufo

The Art of Dialogue Writing   Lesson Six – pg. 31

So, what is too much information? Let me give you an example:

Jill angrily stormed in to the room, slamming the door behind her. "How could you do that to me?" she yelled angrily.

"Just calm down, Jill," Beth said in a way too calm and cool voice. "There's no need to get so upset."

"I am not upset!" Jill yelled, her voice even higher than it was before. "I am furious! I have never been so embarrassed in all my life!" Her blue eyes blazing fire she was so angry.

"I didn't think it was such a big deal. I think you are over reacting as usual," Beth said with boredom, trying to stop Jill's wrath.

"Well it was a big deal to me, Beth!" Jill snapped. "I don't know if I'll ever be able to forgive you!"

"Sure you will," Beth said soothingly, "you always do." She smiled a condescending smile at Jill who was still spitting mad.

"Not this time, Beth!" Jill screeched as she turned to leave the room. "Not this time, not ever again." She was so angry that she couldn't say anymore, she just left.

See the too much information part in that dialogue? It was established right in the first sentence that Jill was mad and in sentence two we saw that Beth was the calm one. Did we need to keep re-establishing it in each and every sentence? Did we need to say who was speaking in each sentence? Probably not. Sure, it makes your word count go up but it gets to be too repetitive and not realistic.

If we were to re-write the scene it would go something like this:

Jill angrily stormed in to the room, slamming the door behind her. "How could you do that to me?"

Just calm down, Jill," Beth said in a soothing voice. "There's no need to get so upset."

"I am not upset! I am furious! I have never been so embarrassed in all my life!" Her blue eyes blazing fire at her friend.

"I didn't think it was such a big deal. I think you are over reacting as usual."

©Stacey Cotrufo

The Art of Dialogue Writing   Lesson Six – pg. 32

>   "Well it was a big deal to me," she snapped. "I don't know if I'll ever be able to forgive you."
>   "Sure you will; you always do." There was condescension laced with the smile Beth gave.
>   "No, not this time. Not this time, not ever again." Without another word, Jill fled the room.

By omitting a couple of phrases, using some pronouns we were able to write a less ridiculous sounding dialogue without some of the obvious descriptions. It makes for a cleaner scene.

Keeping your dialogues and scenes clean and easy to read is your main goal. That's not to say that sometimes your dialogue will require a more "messy" or "ridiculous" tone to it – but that's only if that is what you are going for. Someone who is dramatic and over the top will make outlandish statements and carry on and rarely make sense – but again, if you've set the scene properly and developed your character so that the reader knows this, the scene won't seem chaotic or ridiculous, it will be holding true to the character.

The bottom line is that you want to keep observing those around you to see how normal people act and react during conversations and use those observations in your writing. Every person has something that they do while they are talking. While it is important to include some of those actions/reactions and emotions in your conversations that you write, you do not have to include EVERY action/reaction and emotion in every line. Pick and choose where it is necessary and where it will make the most sense.

©2011 Stacey Cotrufo

The Art of Dialogue Writing

Exercise 6:

Write a ridiculous dialogue with WAY too much information about how your characters are speaking, feeling and what they are doing. Then, re-write the same dialogue in a cleaner fashion – editing out all of the unnecessary information.

_____

_____

_____

_____

_____

_____

_____

_____

_____

_____

_____

_____

_____

©2011 Stacey Cotrufo

The Art of Dialogue Writing   Lesson Six – pg. 34

©2011 Stacey Cotrufo

Emotional Dialogue

Did you just ever have an emotional day? You know, the type of day where everything either makes you angry or makes you cry but either way you end up an emotional wreck that can't put a complete sentence together? Yes you have, admit it!

Well, that is one form of emotional dialogue that we are going to look at today. I don't know what kind of story that you are actually working on and you may be writing a very upbeat story that never needs dialogue like this but in the future, you might.

Just as we've been addressing in previous lessons, when we are writing dialogue we have to set the scene and make the reader feel the emotions that the characters are feeling. With a deeply emotional scene, it isn't always what is being said as much as it is how the person is feeling or what the other character is observing.

Eyes welling with tears, a voice that is shaky when talking, a subdued tone of voice, slumped shoulders, crying…these are just examples of the kind of gestures one would use when writing an emotional scene.

If you are writing your dialogue and one character is observing the other – you need to really think about how a person looks or acts when they are upset. Not everyone cries; not everyone shows outward signs of their being upset but there are usually just a couple of things that would indicate how they're feeling.

Again, it's all in the setting. If you wrote a scene about someone dying then it is going to be obvious why your characters are now upset but you would still have to include some signs of it in your writing – don't just assume that your reader knows it. If a character's feelings get hurt, how would they react? What would they be doing when the person who hurt their feelings comes around to talk to them?

©Stacey Cotrufo

The Art of Dialogue Writing

So much about learning to write good dialogue scenes has to do with you observing those around you and just people watching. The way that you react to things is not the way that everyone else does. Not everyone cries when someone dies. Some people just shut down and show no emotion, others get mad and then there are others who just pretend as if nothing has happened.

This is where your knowing your character will come in to play. The person that you created: how will they react? Are they an emotional person? Are they yellers? Are they quiet? Introspective? Keep to themselves? Drama queen? These are things that you are going to have to decide and keep true to that description.

Here's an example of an emotional scene:

Kim sat quietly in the corner of the room, away from the crowd, staring out the window.

"Hey," a voice next to her whispered. "How are you holing up?"

Looking up, Kim saw that it was her cousin Rachel. Tears welled in her brown eyes. "It's too soon," she said lowly, her voice raw after hours of crying. "It's just too soon for him to be gone."

Rachel sat down on the paisley covered sofa next to her and took Kim's hand. "It always is."

The two sat in silence for a few minutes as tears flowed down Kim's face. "I didn't get there soon enough; he died all alone. He died before I could tell him that I loved him one last time."

Swallowing her own tears, Rachel replied, "He knew, sweetheart. Jeff knew that you loved him." She pulled her cousin close and hugged her as she cried. It was hard to watch someone you loved be in so much pain. If she could, Rachel would take it all away; but she couldn't. God had a plan and although it was hard to tell what that plan was at the moment, she knew she needed to be strong.

"What am I supposed to do now?" Kim's shoulders shook as her sobs wracked her whole body.

"I wish I had the words to tell you, I really do. Unfortunately, all I can say is that you just have to take it one day at a time." Her words were spoken softly and soon Kim raised her head and gave a weak smile.

"Thank you for understanding."

©Stacey Cotrufo

The Art of Dialogue Writing

There were no wild reactions; there was no need for major dramatics. It was a simple scene between two sad relatives. Something else to keep in mind is to stay away from the overuse of exclamation points. In writing it seems like whenever someone wants to show emotion they use exclamation points. Please use them sparingly. No one yells, exclaims, cries all the time in every conversation they have.

Remember that emotional wreck I mentioned at the beginning of the lesson? Their dialogue would probably be a bit rambling and broken up. They would have a lot of sentences that were left hanging and incomplete. Something like this:

"I just don't understand...I mean, it all happened so fast," Kim cried. "I tried, oh, God...I tried to get there...to get to him but I wasn't fast enough!"
Rachel nodded with understanding.
Kim wiped at the tears running down her face. "I wanted to see him...to tell him..." Unable to hold back the sobs that had been threatening to wrack her body, she gave in to them. Rachel hugged her close until her breathing calmed.
"I wanted to tell him...that I loved him just one more time...but it was too late. How can I...he was so young! He was too young to die and I'll never get to tell him how much...he was...I just loved him so much!"

Broken dialogue is acceptable when someone is overwrought with emotion. Think about when you cry and when you are upset. Do all of your sentences make sense? Do you complete every thought? Probably not. It's okay if your character experiences the same thing.

Exercise 7:

I want you to write an emotional dialogue between your two characters. Try to keep it where one is the emotional one and the other is trying to hold it together. They can be emotional about anything but again, make sure that there is enough description and sentences being exchanged to make it interesting.

Make us cry!

©2011 Stacey Cotrufo

The Art of Dialogue Writing

Lesson Seven – pg. 38

The Art of Dialogue Writing   Lesson Eight – pg. 39

Interview with a Friend

It was mentioned in an earlier lesson to not let your voice come through too much in your writing and making sure that all of your characters don't sound like you. Well, for today, this lesson is all about you!

We all have friends and people that we are close with. These are the people that we let ourselves be "real" with – there is no pretending, they love us no matter what and we feel the same way about them. True friends are a blessing.

Up until this point we have been writing using the two characters that you have created. It kind of makes things easier because we control all of their thoughts and actions and basically we have been able to make them do and say whatever we wanted. That is so not the case in the real world.

I love talking on the phone with my friends. We laugh, we joke and we can talk for hours if need be. I'm sure you know what I am talking about. But have you ever sat down and had a serious conversation with a friend? Did you ever talk about maybe something that they did that hurt your feelings or have you ever gotten mad at them and confronted them about it? Not all conversations are happy-go-lucky and filled with laughter.

This lesson will be relatively short. For this lesson you are going to sit down and spend some quality time talking with a friend – preferably face-to-face but if that isn't possible then it can be done over the phone. So far, so good, right?

The important thing is to be true to yourselves. Carry on a conversation like you normally would – do not stage or script a conversation, I want this to be true to you and the relationship that you have with one another. I know it sounds easy but sometimes we want to "fancy it up" and add things to make it sound more interesting. DON'T DO THAT. While we still want significant conversations, it is important that A.) You do not be phony, B.) That you do not let your mom or dads edit it to make it sound better and C.) That you don't try to pick a topic so that you sound more intelligent than you normally are.

©Stacey Cotrufo

The Art of Dialogue Writing

There is no right or wrong conversation to have. However, if you are talking about something of a personal nature, you might not want to share that with the class! Keep it clean, please!

Remember to watch how your friend acts and reacts while they are talking; any gestures that they use but don't STARE and freak them out! Make a mental note to yourself about what they do so that you can maintain a normal conversation.

Exercise 8:

Have a normal conversation with a friend and write it out. Make sure that it is not just a one-word answer type of scenario and that it gives us some sort of insight in to the type of person that you are. Include your own actions, reactions and gestures along with your friend's.

_____

_____

_____

_____

_____

_____

_____

_____

_____

_____

©2011 Stacey Cotrufo

The Art of Dialogue Writing

Lesson Eight – pg. 41

_____

_____

_____

_____

_____

_____

_____

_____

_____

_____

_____

The Art of Dialogue Writing   Lesson Nine – pg. 42

When to Use Dialogue

Have you ever been such good friends with someone that sometimes you could communicate without using words? Well, when you are the writer of a fictional story, you have to remember that while YOU may know what is going on in your character's head, it may not be as obvious to the reader.

Part of writing a good story is finding the right balance between when to describe what is happening and when to let your characters do the talking and sometimes it's hard to figure that out. Something that you need to realize now, early in your writing career, is that even the most skilled of writers, those who have been published dozens of times, still struggle with all of the things that you are struggling with.

The writing process is just that – a process; and it doesn't matter how long you've been doing it, each story is different and presents its own challenges so don't ever let that moment of indecision or confusion stop you from continuing on in your story.

If a story only had dialogue, it would be tedious. If a story only had descriptions of what was going on without any speaking, that would be unrealistic. What you have to do is dig deep in to the story that you want to tell and see what works.

From the website "Daily Writing Tips":

"What proportion of the book can be allotted to atmosphere and characterization compared to plot advancement?

In some genres, the plot may be the most important element. In others, character is of more interest to the reader.

Whatever the genre, however, the story is more than the plot. If your dialog establishes atmosphere and characterization, it will contribute at the same time to the plot.

How much dialog and what kind will be determined by genre and personal style.

©Stacey Cotrufo

The Art of Dialogue Writing

At a guess, I'd think that for most modern writers, the narrative: dialog ratio is about 50:50. Some of the dialog will advance the plot. Some of it will establish character. Ideally, the entire dialog will do some of both.

Since most of us write the kind of books we like to read, it can be helpful to analyze the work of favorite authors to see how they do it. And keep your target audience in mind."

Then I found this on another website geared towards writers:

"The reviewer went on to say that writing a dialogue heavy book made it a simplistic book, an easy read, a lazy effort, an uncomplicated plotline because everyone knows it's the character's inner monologue and descriptions of setting and scene which truly makes a book -- and the characters -- come alive through description, not action.

I think dialogue is incredibly hard to write -- and very hard to write well. Trying to make it read like a conversation, not an info dump, not loading it with tons of dialogue tags which add weight but no meaning, making it a scene that leads to action or carries action. Or using it as an external reveal for the character speaking to make his or her thoughts a public, rather than a private realization, to the reader and the other characters in the scene is difficult to pull off not just once, but throughout the whole of the book. Yes, all the balance of the rest of those elements -- setting, scene, action, internal and external conflict -- make a good book, but amazing dialogue makes a good book a great one.

Creating believable dialogue is not easy by any stretch of the imagination; I know I'm not the only author who strives for authenticity in one page conversations. When dialogue flows, is easy to read and understand, is funny, revealing, poignant, and devastating all in one single sentence, it is exactly the opposite of lazy: it can be sheer poetry."

Okay, so all that being said, we can see that dialogue is not always easy to write but it can be just as important, if not more so, than the descriptions of settings and scenes. I liked the comment from the first website that said that it can be helpful to read books by our favorite authors (if that's who we wish to write like) and use them as a guideline.

©Stacey Cotrufo

The Art of Dialogue Writing   Lesson Nine – pg. 44

For example, there is a certain series of contemporary romances that I enjoy reading and that I really want to write for. All of their books have an extremely similar format. By reading a lot of their books, I learned that format and can now write stories that would fit in to their series. If you have a series that you like or an author that you are fond of and really like their style, read all of their work and see how they do it and what works for them. It's not an exact science but it can really help you to find your balance in the beginning.

In the meantime, I want you to have confidence in your work and know that the only way your writing can be wrong is if it is all dialogue or all descriptive. As long as you incorporate a little bit of both, you are going to be fine.

Exercise 9:

This assignment is going to have three parts but I think you will be able to handle it just fine. The first part: I want you to create a scene for your characters, one where there is no dialogue and it is just you describing their actions/what they are doing.

_____

_____

_____

_____

_____

_____

_____

_____

©Stacey Cotrufo

The Art of Dialogue Writing   Lesson Nine – pg. 45

For the second part, I want you to take that same scene and interject some dialogue between the two of them. Basically you will use all of your describing and your writing from part one and just add dialogue to it.

The Art of Dialogue Writing   Lesson Nine – pg. 46

In the final part I want you to simply use dialogue to tell the whole scene. You are going to simplify the descriptions and let the characters tell what is going on by what they are saying to one another.

_____

_____

_____

_____

_____

_____

_____

_____

_____

_____

_____

_____

_____

_____

_____

_____

©2011 Stacey Cotrufo

The Art of Dialogue Writing   Lesson Ten – pg. 47

The Voices in Your Head: Inner Dialogue

Do you ever find yourself talking to yourself? Or maybe arguing with yourself in your own head? Inner dialogue is often defined as "The sentences that people tell themselves and the debate that often goes on "inside their head" a form of self-talk or inner speech" or "Our inner dialogue, or self-talk, refers to the conversation you have with yourself. Your thoughts. Your thinking process. What's running inside your head the whole time."

We all do it. It's not anything to be ashamed of. Sometimes we are faced with a tough decision to make and there is no one around to help us so we weigh the pros and cons in our head and sort of debate it out with ourselves. Other times we may need to take on a task that has us scared or nervous so we give ourselves an inner pep-talk to build our confidence up.

These are just a few reasons a person would find themselves having an inner dialogue with themselves.

This question was posted on a writing blog that I found: *"How does an author write inner dialogue, that is, when a particular character's thoughts become the dialogue? The character may be making a decision, weighing their options, or making observations that they would not say out loud in the presence of other characters."*

The answers I saw varied all over the place. I have to be honest, I don't think it's that hard of a question nor is it something that is difficult to do. I hope that by the end of the lesson that you will feel the same way, too.

The most obvious thing to avoid when writing inner dialogue: Do not use, *"He though to himself."* Who else is he going to think to? Eliminate the redundancy and simply use, "He thought." Easy, right?

I was trying to find the best way to describe this that would be easy to understand and easy to apply. After writing and rewriting this part of the lesson several times, I decided that this article from Dailywritingtips.com, says it best:

©Stacey Cotrufo

How not to do it
Setting off a character's thoughts in quotation marks is a definite no-no. Such a technique is confusing to the reader. When we see quotation marks, we have the expectation that a character is speaking the words aloud to another person.

Some writers and writer's guides do use or recommend italics to designate thoughts, but the device can be distracting to readers.

Using a different font would make things worse.

Adding **to himself** *to* **he thought** *is redundant.*

How to do it
Sometimes it is necessary to use "he thought," or "she wondered" to avoid confusion, but such tags can be used sparingly.

Okay, so where do I stand on all of this? Personally, I do use italics when I am writing inner dialogue and most books that I've seen have used that. I don't find it distracting and to me, it draws attention to what the character is saying/thinking to himself which is usually key to the story.

But back to concept of inner dialogue itself. Let's spend a few more minutes exploring it. While cruising the internet to work on this lesson, I found this interesting explanation of inner dialogue that I thought would be helpful. This is from a personal excellence blog which really had nothing to do with writing, but the author did focus, for a day, on inner dialogue. I edited it quiet a bit to fit what we are discussing but the points and examples are all valid.

For example, say you're faced with a problem. In just a snap of say maybe 30 seconds, all of this might fly through your mind: "Oh great, not again. Why am I always facing this?" "Let's focus here. What can I do to fix this thing?" "I wonder if Friend X can help me with this. Maybe he will. Maybe he won't because he's too busy." "I could have avoided this if I did X and Y. Sigh." "I feel like going to sleep. Let's do this tomorrow."

©Stacey Cotrufo

The Art of Dialogue Writing

Your self-talk is all the "talking" and "conversing" that you do with yourself, inside your mind, whether it's on an ongoing basis, before you take action or make a decision. Your self-talk makes up your inner reality. It is often said that your external reality is an extension of your inner reality. Without even exploring your self-talk yet, you can guess what's going on the inside just by looking out in your life. If you're one who keeps wanting to lose weight and be fit, but somehow keeps getting off track, you probably have self-talk that goes against your fitness goal. If you want to find your soul mate but you keep ending up with the wrong people, your self-talk is probably not helping you meet Mr/Ms Right. If you wish for financial abundance but you are scrimping from day to day, maybe your self-talk is not conducive to financial abundance to begin with.

A little bit deep, I know, but the points were good ones. Now I'll give you some examples of different ways to include inner dialogue in your writing. All of the examples below are correct ways to indicate internal thought.

"I can't believe my good fortune," Joe thought. "I've won the lottery again!"

Joe couldn't believe his good fortune at winning the lottery not once, but twice.

A winner. Joe stared at his second lottery ticket. *A two-time winner!*

There is more than one correct way to indicate a main character's internal thoughts. Publishers and editors may have different guidelines that they go by. The key is to be consistent. If you decide to use italics rather than quotation marks to indicate thought, use them throughout rather than switching back and forth.

Any of those ways will work and while you may have noticed throughout the lesson there is no one right way to do it. Sometimes it is a personal preference while other times it is dictated by what a specific publisher is looking for.

And just to prove the point further – when I indie published I worked with four separate editors. When I got my book deal and had my publisher's editors go over my work? They corrected everything differently! So just know, there really can be a preference. Go with what you feel is right and you can deal with a publisher's preference later!

©Stacey Cotrufo

The Art of Dialogue Writing   Lesson Ten – pg. 50

Exercise Ten:

I want you to pick one of your characters and write a scene for them that will include several points of them having an internal dialogue. The scene doesn't have to be major but I am looking for several significant sentences (at least ten sentences) so that we understand what is going on and why the character is having the inner dialogue.

_____

_____

_____

_____

_____

_____

_____

_____

_____

_____

_____

_____

©2011 Stacey Cotrufo

The Final Scene

Okay, so for the last ten lessons we have discussed all of the ways (and why) to include dialogue in your writings. We have gone over when there is too much, too little and just the right amount (sounds like the Three Bears, doesn't it?) The rest now, my dear students is up to you. You need to take this information and use it in your stories and use it well.

When it was time for me to write this lesson I realized that by this point, you had all of your information. I had shown you all that you need to know on this level to write some interesting dialogue for your stories. So what do we do for today?

This final lesson is a chance for you to shine. You've written several scenes that have included different types of dialogue and by now you should be able to put your characters in any type of situation or scenario and have them converse appropriately.

So for your final assignment you have two scenes to write – one that exists and one that you create. What does that mean? For your first scene, I want you to pick a movie or a television show that you are familiar with and enjoy and study one scene of dialogue between two characters. Then I want you to write out that scene – imagine that you have written the script and the actors are acting it out. So go ahead and pick your movie or tv show, find a scene and write it out. Then, share what you've written with your parents or a friend and have them critique it for you to see how accurately you portrayed all of the dialogue and the emotion behind it.

The next scene will be one of your own creation. You create the characters and set the scene. It can be anything you want – a drama, a comedy – and any genre you like. The one thing you must do is include plenty of dialogue. Once you've written it out, see if you can get two volunteers to play your characters and see how creatively you showed the emotion behind their conversation. This is a great way to see if what you're writing is actually coming across to your readers.

Are you up for the challenge??

©2011 Stacey Cotrufo

The Art of Dialogue   Lesson Eleven – pg. 54

©2011 Stacey Cotrufo

Congratulations!! You've completed your course on the art of dialogue writing! I hope that you have more confidence in your creative writing and your ability to create interesting dialogue. I look forward to reading your books in the future!

©2011 Stacey Cotrufo

Made in the USA
San Bernardino, CA
13 April 2017